THE DISTANCE
BETWEEN TWO POINTS
IS MEASURED IN MEMORIES,
LABRADOR 1988

D1294316

ISBN 0-920293-23-9

This project is produced by Presentation House Gallery with assistance from the Art Gallery of Memorial University of Newfoundland, Air Canada, The Canada Council, The Newfoundland and Labrador Arts Council, and Multiculturalism Canada.

Presentation House receives annual support from the City of North Vancouver, the District of North Vancouver, the Province of British Columbia through the Ministry of Municipal Affairs, Recreation & Culture, and The Canada Council.

Design/ David Clausen
Photography/ Robert Keziere, installation views & objects.
Printing/Hemlock Printers
Typesetting/Journal of Commerce

A shortened version of the original french text by Jacqueline Fry appeared in *Parachute* No. 57 (January 1990), pp. 35-36.

THE DISTANCE
BETWEEN TWO POINTS
IS MEASURED IN MEMORIES,
LABRADOR 1988

MARLENE CREATES

PRESENTATION
HOUSE
GALLERY

TABLE OF CONTENTS

INTRODUCTION

For over a decade, Marlene Creates has recorded and produced works of art from her gentle interventions in nature. Using paper, photographs, and found materials, she has created pieces which mark her participation in the wilderness, producing *souvenirs* of her acts. Her work has been autobiographical, concerned with human perception of *place* and the role of memory in this relationship. More recently she is involving others in her exploration, executing a ritualistic inquiry into the nature of human identity - its shaping as affected by the land and our recollections of these places which "bear the traces of many imaginings, the scars of conflicting territorial claims, the quirks of an obsessed attention, but . . . have always a conjunction of shapes that is unique to the place". [1]

Creates has written about her work: "I am interested in the relationship between human experience and the landscape and, in particular, the ways in which the landscape is richly and profoundly differentiated into *places*. How do we distinguish one place from another? What constitutes a landmark? How do different people perceive the same area of land? What points do they remember? These are some of the questions I have been considering in my work". A portion of the most recent body of work, produced in Labrador, was exhibited at Presentation House Gallery from March 2 to April 1, 1990. The publication is produced on the occasion of this exhibition and includes the complete suite of eighteen works.

I would like to thank all of the project's sponsors, listed elsewhere in these pages, and particularly the Art Gallery of Memorial University of Newfoundland for their special assistance. Thanks are also due to Diane Evans and Cherie Markiewicz at Presentation House Gallery, and Robert Keziere, David Clausen, Jacqueline Fry and Elizabeth Ritchie, for their valuable contributions to the catalogue. Finally, we are most grateful to Marlene for her resourcefulness and support of the project.

Karen Love
Director/Curator

1 Don Lyn Lyndon, *Places*, The MIT Press, Cambridge, Volume 4, Number 1, 1987

The Distance Between Two Points is Measured in Memories, Labrador 1988 constitue pour Marlene Creates une étape majeure dans le développement d'un travail que la typologie historique de l'art classe dans la catégorie du *Land Art* (sans doute devrions-nous dire *Art in the Land*).

Il y a dix-huit assemblages dans cette série, chacun contenant quatre images : la photographie d'une personne âgée dans une cuisine ou salon; une carte géographique dessinée; un texte imprimé en caractères sansérifs; et enfin la photographie d'un site. Tous les formats sont identiques (28x36 cm). Les deux images photographiques, la carte dessinée et le texte produisent l'effet quelque peu abstrait de deux tableaux blancs entre deux tableaux noirs. Par terre, à l'avant de chaque série, à l'exception de cinq, est déposé un objet d'origine ''naturelle'' (d'ordre minéral ou végétal), à la façon d'une marque vivante et/ ou d'un indice discret. Le déploiement mural des séquences imagées et les petites masses au sol provoquent une sensation d'intimité quelque peu austère et invitent à l'observation non superficielle.

Marlene Creates nomme justement ces séries des *memory maps*, cartes-mémoires d'habitants de communautés de type récemment urbanisées du Nord Labrador : Inuit, Naskapi Innu et colons d'origine euro-canadienne. Il s'agit de ce qui est resté gravé dans leur mémoire d'un lieu de vie passé, et qu'ils expriment par un dessin et par un récit. Parallèlement, celui ou celle qui possède cette mémoire a été photographié par Marlene Creates dans l'espace quotidien de vie actuelle qu'il ou elle a choisi d'occuper pour la prise de vue; l'espace-souvenir est représenté tel que son appareil photographique l'a surpris en 1988. Les objets posés sur le sol (bûches, bois hérissé d'un clou, bloc de granit veiné noir et rose, fragment de pierre de Labrador, brique de terre moussue, boule de pierre grise . . .) sont là parce que mentionnés dans le récit, acteurs naguère vivants du lieu-souvenir et non simulacres de témoins originels pour galerie d'art.

Ainsi confrontés à dix-huit cartes-mémoires, nous partageons à la fois dix-huit destins et l'aventure esthétique et éthique de l'artiste qui franchit pour un grand nombre de visiteurs potentiels le cap de l'indifférence ou de l'ignorance. Si la mémoire s'exerce chez Clara ou Jim Voisey, Joe Ford, Josephine Kalleo, Sam Winters, Hilda ou John Dickers, Philip Hunter ou Sybilla Nitsman, Rosie ou Chesley Webb ou encore Chesley et George Flowers, Gilbert Rich, Joachim Nui, Mary Ann Noah, Bert Saunders et Sidney Dicker, c'est que le passage d'un style de vie à un autre éclaire et rend sublimes les images du passé. Le territoire de chasse, de pêche et de piégeage, l'espace domestique et celui de collecte sauvage redeviennent, dans les paroles et les lignes dessinées, des lieux réels, libres et chaleureux. Sidney Dicker se souvient de Nain : ''This place here at one time was all green with lots of little flowers. We call them buttercups those little yellow flowers. And all the little brooks were clean. But since they started building, it's ruined. When it blows hard we get a lot of sand.''

Les séries assemblées ne sont pas simples à approcher. Chaque catégorie d'images (le lieu domestique, la carte, le texte, le site), tout en proposant chacune un univers spécifique, est indissociable des autres. L'oeil procède à une sorte de va-et-vient en filigrane bien que fixé sur une image. Marlene Creates réussit à nous faire partager le mouvement de mémoires anciennes, attachées à leurs sources pré-urbaines, mémoires faussement comprises comme en marge des nôtres et pourtant si proches!

La photographie du lieu domestique expose les supports matériels — fonctionnels et décoratifs — de la vie quotidienne: la cuisinière, le réfrigérateur, le poêle, la table avec sa nappe, les étagères murales, l'armoire à épices, la commode, la télé, le transistor . . . Les ustensiles domestiques sont visibles: casseroles, plats, assiettes, tasses, cafetière . . . Le surplus ornemental se déploie: pots de plantes, fleurs séchées, calendriers, cartes, boîtes, bibelots figuratifs . . . D'innombrables photographies familiales, dont les formats et les cadres pourraient fournir la preuve d'un jeu sur les variations plastiques, tapissent les murs et se dressent sur des étagères interrompues par l'horloge murale ou sur pied au statut esthétique ambigu qui marque le temps à présent piégé seconde par seconde mais se laisse aimer comme objet. Ces dispositifs de quelques intérieurs de maisons à Nain, Davis Inlet, et Hopedale sont conformes à ceux qu'on trouve dans les résidences ou appartements des strates dites ''populaires'' dans les agglomérations urbanisées de la planète. [1] J'aimerais prendre plus de temps à reconnaître et situer chaque objet, mais pour Marlene Creates les images ne sont pas rassemblées afin de constituer des exemples d'une quelconque sociologie du goût; elles sont là, témoins d'une tranformation bouleversante dont nous découvrons les aspects en parcourant les séquences. Tous ces arrangements qui visent un confort sédentaire ne nous masquent pas certaines ambiguïtés désolantes de la situation. Gilbert Rich par exemple, un habitant d'origine innu du nouveau Davis Inlet a choisi de se montrer debout à côté de son poêle, un récipient probablement plein d'eau à la main. Il sourit, contraint ou moqueur? L'eau, il faut aller la chercher au dehors. . .[2]

Les cartes dessinées suivent les photographies des personnes à l'intérieur. Ce qui nous touche et nous fascine dans ces cartes provient probablement de ce qui, au-delà du témoignage particulier et intense auquel nous sommes confrontés, constitue les qualités émotives et esthétiques propres à la cartographie. Ce sont des qualités sensibles tout au long de son développement historique même lorsque les aspects illustratifs (paysages, êtres humains, choses. . .) seront peu à peu abandonnés. Ces qualités nous paraissent provenir d'une volonté archaïque de construire les traces exactes d'un itinéraire tout en inventant, au fur et à mesure, des signes conventionnels et abstraits. L'oscillation entre la représentation picturale et l'abstraction persiste. Ces cartes dessinées sont à la fois des mémoires et des créations imaginaires.

Les dix-huit cartes-mémoires des personnes âgées avec lesquelles l'artiste a entretenu des conversations ressemblent (pour nous) à de fragiles constructions linéaires sur espaces blancs connotant l'infini.[3] Mais ce fond rectangulaire blanc en papier a servi de support à un espace très localisé. Ce que nous prenons pour l'infini ne sont que les entours d'un lieu auquel la mémoire donne des dimensions à la fois agrandies et précises. C'est un lieu-parcours. C'est l'océan, c'est le territoire de pêche. Ce sont les terrains de chasse au caribou, au renard, au vison, mais également ceux de la récolte du bois. C'est la côte découpée et les petites îles dont on connaît les noms, la plupart inuktitut. Ce sont enfin les maisons familiales et voisines. Les collines, les bois, les roches, sont absorbés par les lignes qui dessinent les rapports entre la terre et l'eau. Comme dans une exposition de groupe de peintures expressionnistes abstraites, les cartes-tableaux, à première vue, déploient leurs similitudes pour se distinguer ensuite dès qu'on les observe. Certaines sont complexes et semblent restituer les aventures d'une géographie, d'autres sont minimales et signalent d'un fil continu et ténu des morceaux d'espaces réduits. Certaines plus illustratives s'abandonnent aux illusions de la représentation picturale. L'écriture intervient parfois au secours de la mémoire.

La pratique cartographique fait partie de l'univers graphique des Inuit. Sans se tourner vers les figurations topographiques traditionnelles pré-historiques et en ne tenant compte que des dessins géographiques conservés, publiés ou exposés depuis la fin du siècle dernier, l'adresse des habitants du monde arctique à se situer entre les quatre points cardinaux est bien connue. Robin McGrath a bien raison de rappeler à ce sujet les expériences de Franz Boas et de Robert Flaherty. [4] Il associe notamment la renaissance actuelle de la cartographie inuit aux négociations suscitées par leurs revendications territoriales : ''(which) have required the knowledge and expertise of Inuit elders in documenting land use and occupancy by producing maps to show traditional hunting areas, animal migration routes, sea-ice trails and seasonal habitations.'' [5] Des projets d'étude des modes d'occupation des terres ont été initiés depuis 1973 non seulement chez les Inuit mais entre autres, également, chez les colons et les Naskapi-Montagnais du Labrador. [6]

Le danger serait d'*ethniciser* ces représentations de l'espace. Ce qui a frappé

Marlene Creates, c'est qu'il n'est pas possible, *pour le moment*, d'attribuer certains dessins à des auteurs inuit, d'autres à des Innu et enfin d'autres encore à des Settlers''. Le déploiement de contours, les isolements de petites masses, les effets de continuité, le minimalisme ou l'effort pour détailler, semblent, à une exception près, avoir plutôt à faire avec le genre qu'avec la spécificité ethnique. Pour toutes les mémoires transférées hors des lieux de leur enfance (et pour plusieurs, de leur temps d'adulte) ce qui constitue la substance même de leurs souvenirs c'est la géographie et le travail. Les distinctions semblent issues de pratiques dont la plupart sont communes soit aux hommes, soit aux femmes. L'espace masculin (à l'exception de celui de Bert Saunders qui décrit soigneusement l'ancien Davis Inlet autour du poste de la compagnie de la Baie d'Hudson dirigé par son père et son grand-père) se confond surtout avec l'extension du territoire de chasse et de pêche. Ils dessinent le long parcours des terres et des eaux. L'espace féminin tend à se réduire à celui d'un territoire marqué par des activités ordonnées autour de la maison ou géographiquement plus limitées.

La carte annonce ou double le texte qui la suit. Elle visualise la narration et trace la vie. Le texte, lui, remplace la voix. Dans la froideur de son lettrage, il nous retient par ses contradictions. Il est à la fois vestige d'une voix et lettres mortes! Mais l'unité des quatre images nous impose la présence du narrateur. Les lieux auxquels la carte donnait une existence sont racontés, ou plutôt, les deux opérations sont solidaires et le texte pourrait précéder la carte. Jim Voisey raconte et nous lisons, "Now this will be The Bay. . . Nineteen miles of it. . . Island here. Island there. Tabor Island where they gets the Labradorite from. . . You'll see what they call Brown's River. But it's only a little brook. . . This would be Garland Bight. . . This is a hill. . . Now off of the Harbour there's islands. One, two, three. . .''

Rosie Webb, de son côté, concentre son espace : "Old man's house here. Path up to our house. And Jim's house up here. Our house. And Ronald's. And Henry's little old house there. . .''

Les dernières images des séries sont celles des lieux-souvenirs. Ce sont les photographies prises par Marlene Creates lors d'une seconde étape voyageuse au-delà des trois villages obligatoires vers les espaces indiqués par la mémoire. Il s'agissait de parcourir l'itinéraire dessiné et de retrouver les points sensibles de la cartographie. Il y a certainement là une expérience qui se situe au coeur même de l'oeuvre qu'elle nous présente. La carte et la narration fixée par le texte reprennent vie dans le site visité, et à la mémoire de ses anciens habitants se substitue la mémoire d'un visiteur compréhensif et inquiet.

Pour le regardeur des images dans la galerie, les étendues d'eau, les découpages de la terre, les dispositifs rocheux, les masses boisées, les collines, le ciel, les lignes d'horizon, les îles minuscules, et les maisons abandonnées, répondent aux chambres équipées de Nain, Davis Inlet et Hopedale. Les objets déposés au sol — le morceau de pierre de Labrador devant la série de Jim Voisey, l'encadrement de boutons d'or séchés dans la série de Sidney Dicker, ou la brique de terre moussue devant la série de Rosie Webb - semblent échappés du texte et de la photo-souvenir.

Les dix-huit cartes-mémoires du Labrador datant de 1988 ne sont pas les premières exposées. En 1987 à Sault-Sainte-Marie, sous le même titre, Marlene Creates présentait quatre assemblages réunis à partir des expériences de personnes âgées (femmes et hommes) de la région, certaines d'origine ojibwa.[7] Montrés à l'extérieur, les assemblages exposaient la carte-mémoire gravée sur une plaque d'ardoise à partir du dessin. Une autre version de la même série était plus tard montrée à Ottawa.[8] Enfin les dix-huit cartes-mémoires du Labrador étaient présentées à St. John's.[9]

Si ces cartes-mémoires marquent un tournant décisif dans le travail de Marlene Creates *Land Art Artist*, il faudrait préciser en quoi consiste ce tournant et se demander s'il ne s'agirait pas d'un développement plus général de cette form d'art peut-être révélateur d'options nées du temps présent?

Le voyage du Labrador consolide le projet de Sault-Sainte-Marie et met fin en quelque sorte aux parcours naturalistes à interventions discrètes dans le paysage qui ont caractérisé la trajectoire de l'artiste entre 1979 et 1987. [10] C'était une trajectoire marquée par des explorations solitaires de géographies et de géologies au cours desquelles les indices esthétiques de sa présence désindividualisée étaient captés photographiquement et organisés visuellement dans le respect dû au souvenir et dans l'inquiétude des ambiguïtés de sa reproduction : application éphémère de papier de riz, transport de roches et de pierres, aplatissement d'herbes folles par son corps ensommeillé, jet nocturne d'une pierre dans l'eau. . . ''Le paysage est important pour moi, mais encore plus importante est l'idée qu'il devient un lieu parce que quelqu'un y est passé'' dit-elle déjà en 1985 à propos de son projet *Traverser deux rivières: des lieux, des sentiers, des souvenirs*. [11] Elle annonce ainsi, nous semble-t-il, qu'à sa relation personnelle avec l'environnement (vu comme l'univers, ou comme le cosmos) va se substituer l'expérience de *quelqu'un* dans les lieux (vus comme des espaces habités par des vies humaines).

Il ne peut être question ici d'entrer dans la complexité idéologique des diverses catégories de *Land Art*, [12] mais on pourrait peut-être situer le travail de Marlene Creates dans une strate typologique qui comporterait, entre autres, les oeuvres de Richard Long et celles de Hamish Fulton que Mark Rosenthal classe respectivement le premier dans la catégorie ''Modest Gestures in the Landscape'' et le second dans celle de ''Idealized Landscape''. [13] Dans ces expériences la ''Nature'' est peu, à peine, ou pas touchée et la lente et longue circulation du corps sur la terre crée une sorte de communion (ou reconstruit des relations perdues!) entre le site et le marcheur amoureux et pensif.

Il nous semble que les voyages solitaires actuels de Marlene Creates signalent une transformation de ces perspectives. De façon générale, dans de nombreuses activités du *Land Art* depuis une vingtaine d'années, il s'agissait plutôt de fonder des expériences plastiques à partir d'attitudes culturelles vis-à-vis d'une nature appréhendée comme paysage. L'être humain n'apparaissait que dans ses traces : traces archaïques (monuments) ou traces fabriquées par l'artiste lui-même. Marlene Creates cesse aujourd'hui d'être le témoin privilégié parce qu'elle rencontre des témoins plus pertinents et rarement consultés. Si elle décide d'écouter les personnes âgées du Labrador, c'est que leur expérience — le passage d'un mode de vie inscrit dans le paysage à celui d'une participation devenue obligatoire à un mode de vie urbanisé — donne vie et sens à ces ''relations perdues'' avec le temps et l'espace que certains *land artists* traquaient.

A la veille des années 90, dans un contexte où les transformations écologiques menaçantes sont devenues objets d'information et d'expérimentation quotidiennes et où, parallèlement, les forteresses culturelles occidentales semblent assiégées non pas, dans le meilleur des cas, par d'autres idéologies dominantes mais par des unités humaines en quête d'une construction équilibrée, il serait intéressant de découvrir si des voies nouvelles ont été empruntées par certains *land artists* des années 60 et 70. Il n'est pas impossible que quelques trajectoires persistent, à peine modifiées, parce qu'elles se sont avérées avec le temps d'une qualité et d'une pertinence inaltérables. [14] Par ailleurs certaines oeuvres réalisées déjà dans les jeunes années du *land art* pourraient parfaitement être créées aujourd'hui sous la pression des événements actuels. Un bon exemple, nous semble-t-il, serait *Time Landscape* d'Alan Sonfist, commencé en 1965. [15]

Aujourd'hui Marlene Creates a choisi un parcours esthétique qui valorise les habitants du site choisi et c'est leur mémoire qu'elle pose au centre d'une expérience de l'environnement.

Mais elle ne fait pas que cela. Marlene Creates parcourt et nous fait connaître des lieux plus ou moins associés à un scandale qui provient à la fois du fait colonial en tant que tel et de l'exercice d'un marketing post-industriel des ressources de la terre. Parmi les Innu de la péninsule Québec-Labrador n'y a-t-il pas des chasseurs qui ont continué une vie nomade traditionnelle et dont les droits légaux n'étaient pas reconnus par un gouvernement qui, en 1970, construisait, sans dialogues préalable compensations ultérieures réelles, un réservoir inondant leurs territoires de survie? e sommes-nous pas proches ou même à l'intérieur de *Nitassinan* (Our Land) cet space soumis aux vols supersoniques et à basse altitude de jets militaires entraînant à partir de la base de l'OTAN à Goose Bay?

En considérant les lieux-souvenirs et en re-parcourant la distance qui les sépare es cuisines et salles à manger d'aujourd'hui, le spectateur ne peut échapper aux pressantes réflexions que l'exposition de Marlene Creates veut faire naître grâce à une mise en ordre visuelle claire et discrète, caractéristique de son art. Ces images ont la valeur d'un partage.

Jacqueline Fry

TES

Nous pensons irrésistiblement au narrateur d'un roman de minique Fernandez qui se rappelle le jour où un camarade de ée l'emmena chez lui ''. . . un trois pièces propre et soigné du té de Javel. La famille se tenait dans la cuisine-salle à manger, tour d'une table ronde couverte d'une toile cirée à fleurs. . . Moi i avait grandi au milieu des livres je n'aperçus au mur que des tes postales, un coucou suisse, le calendrier des postes. . .'' *Etoile Rose*, Grasset, 1978, p. 41).

Dans une autre photographie, Joachim Nui a monté sa tente rs l'avant de sa maison. Là, dit-il, il peut retrouver la fraîcheur qui manque et l'odeur des branches d'épinette qui tapissent le sol sa tente. Cette fois le lieu actuel et le lieu souvenir se confondent ns une tentative de correction de l'ordre nouveau.

Nous écrivons ''a entretenu des conversations'' et non ''a estionné'', car il ne s'agit nullement d'une expérience nspiration sociologique. Nous sommes sans doute ici plus près une expérience d'ordre anthropologique. Il faudrait se livrer à de vantes et peut-être utiles distinctions entre: anthropologue-nnologue, anthropologue, artiste-anthropologue, artiste tout court!

Robin McGrath, ''Maps as Metaphor: One hundred years of Inuit ctography,'' *Inuit Art Quarterly*, Spring 1988,Vol.3, Nov. 1, p.6.

Ibid., p.6.

6. Hugh Brody, *Maps and Dreams: A Journey into the Lives and Lands of the Beaver Indians of North West Canada*, chapitre 10, ''The Indians' Maps''.

7. *The Distance Between Two Points is Measured in Memories, Sault Ste. Marie 1987*, ''Sans Démarcation'', project d'échange culturel Québec-Ontario, Sault-Sainte-Marie, Ontario (avec la participation de la Art Gallery of Algoma et Visual Arts Ontario) 1987.

8. Galerie 101, octobre 1987.

9. *Maskunow: A Trail A Path*, Art Gallery of Memorial University of Newfoundland, 24 février-9 avril 1989, une exposition de groupe préparée par Joan Borsa (incluait six cartes-mémoires du Labrador, trois séries féminines et trois séries masculines); *The Distance Between Two Points is Measured in Memories, Labrador 1988*, Eastern Edge Gallery, 9 avril-25 mai, 1989 (incluait douze cartes-mémoires de la série).

10. Dans *Overlay: Contemporary Art and the Art of Prehistory*, Pantheon Books, New York, 1983, traitant des altérations de mégalithes Lucy R. Lippard cite et illustre *Paper Over the Turlough Hill Cairn, Ireland 1981* de Marlene Creates. Lucy R. Lippard insiste dans sa note sur le mythe local qui donne au lieu sa spécificité archaïque mais les préoccupations de l'artiste étaient ailleurs.

11. Axe Néo-7, Hull, Québec.

12. Voir à ce sujet Alan Sonfist ed. *Art in the Land: A Critical Anthology of Environmental Art*, E. P. Dutton Inc., New York, 1983, 274 p.

13. Ibid., pp. 66 et 68.

14. Heidi Geraets qui a entrepris une thèse de maîtrise: *Back to Nature? Land Reclamation and/or Nature Valorization* est confrontée à ces questions en particulier en travaillant sur les travaux plus récents de Nancy Holt, Robert Morris, et Michael Singer. Elle attire notre attention sur une série de travaux sur papier de Richard Long, *Untitled* (1987). ''His *Untitled* works show a series of footsteps spiralling inward from the edge of the paper until they reach the centre, from where they have nowhere to go.'' (John Grande, ''Art in the Environment'', *Discussion*, Printemps 1989, Vol.8, No.1, p.8, Montreal). Il faut savoir qu'il s'agit d'empreintes de ses pieds chaussés de bottes qui ont été plongées dans la boue polluée d'une rivière!

15. Alan Sonfist a recréé un fragment de forêt de type pré-colonial, c'est-à-dire avant la colonisation de l'Amérique du Nord, en plantant un large rectangle d'espèces d'arbres autochtones sur la place de la Guardia, dans Manhattan, à New York.

Unless otherwise noted, works are courtesy the artist.

*Asterixed titles represent works exhibited at Presentation
 House Gallery, March 2 to April 1, 1990.

STATEMENT

I have been working on the relationship between human experience and the landscape. For the past 10 years I have worked in remote areas where most of my projects and landworks were related to the "natural" aspects of the sites. Then I became interested in what we would call the "cultural": the people who have lived closest to these places. I began to understand that there are certain things about their lives which are being left behind—certain things that matter to them, their experiences of the world which are so different from my own. From these encounters with elderly country people I developed the works which are titled *The Distance Between Two Points is Measured in Memories*

These assemblages include a photograph of the person, some of the story they told me (in their own words), and a "memory map" they drew for me of how they remember their environment. I follow these maps to see the places they have described, and then photograph one of the landmarks on the map and collect, where appropriate, an object from the landscape. The most recent assemblages are from Northern Labrador where I met elderly people from the three different groups who live there: the native Inuit and Naskapi Innu, and the Euro-Canadians who are called Settlers in Labrador.

Most of their stories (native and Settlers) revolve around a sadness at the loss of nature in their lives, now that they live in communities. The increasing urbanization of the world worries me and it was in meeting these people that I got the greatest sense that something has been lost in the way we live now. I don't want to suggest that their lives are romantic; no one would wish that traditional peasant life continue exactly as it was. But these people make sense of their place in nature.

It seems to me now that the ideological distinctions we (western industrial society) have made between nature and culture have separated us from the non-human part of the world, reinforcing the idea that nature exists separate from us. This has brought me to the belief that there needs to be a re-connection between what is experienced as culture and what is experienced as nature.

Marlene Creates,
St. John's, Newfoundland, 1989

Rosie Webb, Labrador 1988*
assemblage of photographs, memory map,
story, and blackberry sod.

I had ten boys and one girl. I had fifteen altogether. Some of them is dead. I don't know how many grandchildren. I never counted. I stayed up there in Webb's Bay ever since I got married. When we got married there was only one house, his father's house. That old house is still up. Log house. Smokehouse and everything up there. Smokes char. Use what they call blackberry leaves. Cuts out square pieces of sod. It was a boat, half a boat. Just the top of a boat put on the ground. Old man's house here. Path up to our house. And Jim's house up here. Our house. And Ronald's. And Henry's little old house there. It's old that smokehouse. Way over a hundred years it must be now. Still uses it. Still good.

 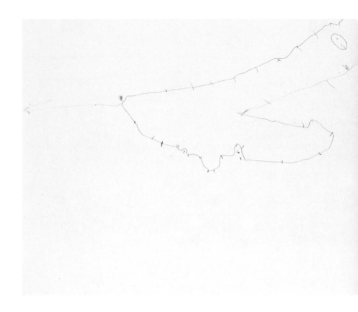

Chesley Webb, Labrador 1988*
assemblage of photographs, memory map,
story, and sand.

That's where the house is, in The Bay. Webb's Bay they call it. Starting around here, close to it anyway, all that shore was all traps. All around there was full of traps. You'd place them so far apart. Couldn't do it all in one day. We'd do this shore one day, then the next day you'd do the other shore. And then the next day up this way, across the land. Then it would be time to see the others again. That used to be hard too. You'd leave, dark in the morning, get back at ten o'clock at night. Walking all day. Foxes and mink. Start fishing after break-up. It's all sand. You wouldn't believe how deep that harbour was. The tide takes it. It fills up every deep place. Now you can't anchor a boat there low tide. It's all sand. Now it's hard for me to get the boat in.

Sidney Dicker, Labrador 1988
assemblage of photographs, memory map,
story, and buttercups.

When I was a young man I got married to an Inuk woman, forty years ago. I have twenty-two grandchildren. The hardest of all was having no father to teach me the things I wanted to know. Hunting and fishing. If I had to live it over, I'd live it all over the same way again. But I wouldn't want to go through losing a son again. Nain was only a little small community at one time. The centre of town those days was the church. Close to the beach. One bad thing they got done here now is building up the place. This place here at one time was all green with lots of little flowers. We call them buttercups those little yellow flowers. And all the little brooks were clean. But since they started building it's ruined. When it blows hard we get a lot of sand.

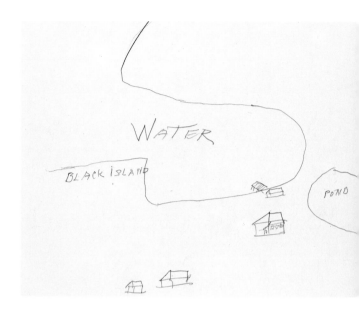

WATER

BLACK ISLAND

POND

Joe Ford, Labrador 1988
assemblage of photographs, memory map,
story, and boulder.

I lived out on an island. Black Island. All the time. Still there, house on Black Island. Belongs to my son now. I don't own anything there any more. Up where my house is there's boulders you know. You'll like it. It's a beautiful place. I used to make beer you know. Rhubarb beer. Boy that's beautiful. The rhubarb grew right in front of the house, right under the window. I used to bottle it up. Whatever kind of bottle I could get. I used to see a lot of schooners from Twillingate and all those places. I used to entertain the Newfies. I played the squeeze box too. We used to have some fun you know. I was prepared. When I saw a schooner come in, I had the beer all ready. Anything for a bit of fun. I don't think about it much. I've got to be happy wherever I am.

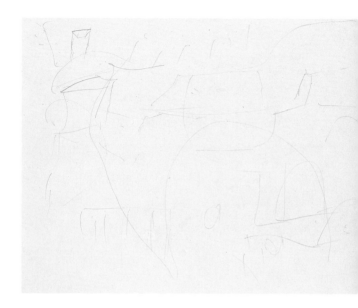

Clara Voisey, Labrador 1988*
assemblage of photographs, memory map,
story, and rock.

That's the house, the one my parents moved in after Jim got married. There was a little smokehouse here by the house. That's the new place. The last place. The last time when I was up there when my parents were still alive, they were in that house. I was up there twice and scrubbed it up. It was white with green edges. The harbour, that's the harbour and the rocks. We had gardens of course. Cabbage and turnips. Two kinds of turnips, yellow and white. Potatoes. We had potatoes all up inside of a hill once. Long ways. We used to have them in by the house too but the ground wasn't that good. Enough for a taste. This stove was in that house.

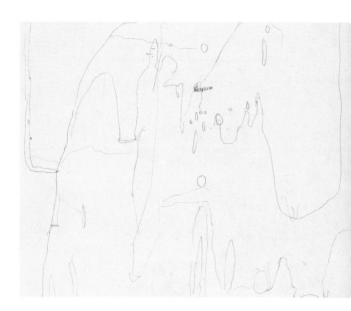

Jim Voisey, Labrador 1988
assemblage of photographs, memory map,
story, and Labradorite.
Collection: Canada Council Art Bank.

Now this will be The Bay. The Bay means from Kamarsuk right up to the bottom of it. That's The Bay. Nineteen miles of it. That's home. They say Voisey's Bay. All I ever called it was home. That's where all of us was born, every one of us was born in that harbour. I think there was fourteen of us lived. One little girl, fifteenth, died. Island here. Island there. Tabor Island where they gets the Labradorite from. That's Kamarsuk. The Winters used to live there. From Kamarsuk you'll see what they call Brown's River. But it's only a little brook, somebody misnamed that. Cabot's Lake River. Kogaluk. It means Big River. It goes way inland. This would be Garland Bight. Then Little Bight. Bob's Cove. Little Spring Cove. Garden Island. The Harbour. Bar Island. Edmund's Point and Edmund's Neck. This is a hill. Joe's Nob is what we calls that. Now off of the Harbour there's islands. One, two, three. Cuff Island. And Outer Island. And Water Island. It's called Water Island because that's where we used to have to fetch water from in the summertime, in a small boat. You'll see some points I haven't got marked on there.

EVEOGATSAJAK

Josephine Kalleo, Labrador 1988*
assemblage of photographs, memory map,
story, and salt-water grass.
Collection: Art Gallery of Memorial
University of Newfoundland.

I was born here, 1920. That's my home. Really home. Right different now. I miss lots of it. Right changed. When I was small I cooked everything outdoors, outside the house. Not allowed a fire outside now, not here in Nain. Everything gone. Codfish and caplin and bakeapple. Everything gone. I make a little box with that green stuff in the fall. In October. My father's sisters taught me when I was ten years old how to. Grows right alongside the water. The green stuff. I pick them up when they are white. They get that colour. They're green now. It's green in the summer. Called Eveogatsajak in Inuktitut. I pick them up in October and put them in a pillowcase. Make them wet in water, and then sewing that.

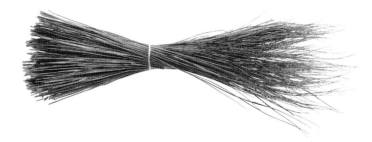

Sam Winters, Labrador 1988*
assemblage of photographs, memory map,
and story.

Used to be a fine old place. Kamarsuk. Three houses. But
there was a lot of people when we were all together. We
used to wear mostly skin clothes them days, right to the
mitts and everything. We mostly growed up on meat such
as caribou, seal meat, birds, stuff like that. If I was smarter
like I was them days, I wouldn't be here. I'd be home. But
I can't do nothing now. I got to be here. I finds it bad now
sitting around like this every day. I used to go all around
to those places by dog team. All of it. Everything. Now out
here there was three little small islands, one after the
other, right in the middle of the run. We used to go this
way to go home. Long ways off. About twenty-two miles.
It would only be like a cloud when you were there looking
at the homeland. You could hardly make out the old hill.
Like a cloud.

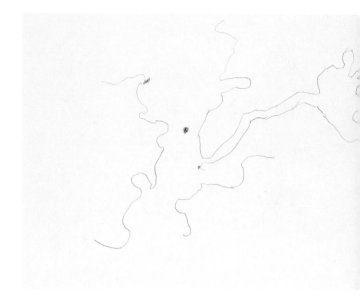

Gilbert Rich, Labrador 1988
assemblage of photographs, memory map,
story, and wood.

I was born in Utshimasits. That's the one, you know, the old place. Island over here. And then over here right in there, that's the old place, Old Davis Inlet. That's where I was born, 1931, something like that. Naskapi Indians is what they call us. Mushuau Innu is what we call ourselves. In the winter we went in the country. Inside you know. About August everybody went in the country. Pulled it you know, had to use the canoe. Got to stay in there all winter. Hunt caribou, fox, anything. Mink, otter. And then come out all people in June. Summer got to work at the fish and wood. Get wood. Got to use an axe. And a bucksaw. And some use a chain saw. All place, lots of wood. Two days now didn't make a fire. Nobody to give me wood.

Joachim Nui, Labrador 1988*
assemblage of photographs, memory map,
story, and boughs.

Always lived in tent. First time Innu people were staying in a house was 1967. That's Davis Inlet. After that people stopped going in the country, stopped taking their families. 1966 was the last time I went in the country with the whole family. After that I got a job. Now it's only sometimes for two or three days for caribou hunting. I like sometime to stay in the tent. Don't like to stay in the house all the time. In the wintertime when the boughs get dry, never take it out. Just put new ones on top. In the summertime not the same thing. When it gets dry, take it out and put new ones. Every week put new ones. Shitats. That means boughs. Three kinds of boughs we use in the tent. Girls get the boughs in the woods. That's girls' job. Always like that, girls and women. My two daughters and four more girls got these boughs yesterday. Six girls.

Mary Ann Noah, Labrador 1988*
assemblage of photographs, memory map,
story, and burnt rock.
Collection: Art Gallery of Memorial
University of Newfoundland.

When I was in the country I stayed in a tent. Fall, winter, spring, then summer. Me and my mother and my father and my brothers. The Hudson's Bay here. The store manager's house. This house is the first one, the one in Old Davis Inlet. The warehouse. Another warehouse. I don't know how many. Two or three I think. Our church. It's not in there no more. When the people died they go up here. My mother's buried up there. We put our tent handy to the church. If you go down there now, you can see where they put the tents. Looks old. Rocks in a circle outside tent. Make a fire to make some tea and fry fish.

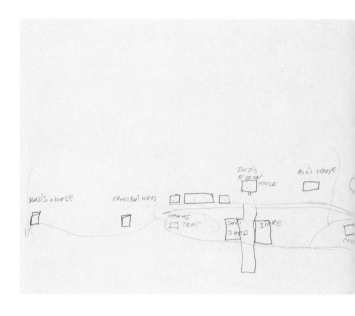

Bert Saunders, Labrador 1988*
assemblage of photographs, memory map,
story, and log with bolt.

I've got a grandmother, my father and my oldest brother buried over there. I was born there. Old Davis Inlet. That's my old stomping ground. The Indians used to put their tents all along here right down to the church. From June or whenever they got out of the country until August. There may be twelve, fifteen, maybe twenty tents depending on how many came out of the country. All that's left there now is just Dad's new house. And the graveyard. That was the store manager's house for the Hudson's Bay. It was called The Post. Wasn't very much in that store though. All the store and all the house and the church were connected by a wooden walkway. It was made out of logs bolted together. You just go inside there yet and there's giant size trees. That's where they got all the wood. They sawed all their own lumber.

Sybilla Nitsman, Labrador 1988
assemblage of photographs, memory map,
and story.

They brought us here from Okak, 1918, 1919. I was six, going seven. Because the flu was on. In the Harmony. That's the big old boat. Three masts. I was only seventeen when I married first. He died around 1940 I suppose. He got that pneumonia. No doctors here then. My children were all kind of small. Seven children. Five boys and two girls, and two little boys dead. And when he died I was thinking what am I going to do with my children now. Then I married to a man from here Hopedale. My children were grown up by then. I adopted two, too. When I was young like you I never thought I would be an old woman. I came here to this house in 1948. The old mission house is there. The ministers and storekeepers were all in there. They had families, lots of families. And the church here now. My house. Not too long, not too big. Right handy to the church. I can make sealskin boots yet. I'm right happy to do them yet. We used to sew with the lamp in the night. We had to make them, they had no shoes, no rubbers, nothing like that. We never thought this was hard. Only now when we think about what we done. You just do it, do it, what you can.

Philip Hunter, Labrador 1988*
assemblage of photographs, memory map,
story, and rock.

Hopedale. All kinds of islands out there. Lots of islands everywhere. Everywhere. All them islands have names, most of them Inuktitut. We used to fish in every place. All the little islands. Spread them all out on the rock. That's all we used to have. When they were half dry, turn them over. Long time to dry them up, three or four weeks sometimes, because we used to get bad weather sometimes. When the storm was coming on, we had to take them up and put them in one place, pile them up. Fish used to come around July fifteenth. Lots of ice still then. I remember because my birthday is July fifteenth. That's why I remember. I used to have some fish for my birthday.

John Dickers, Labrador 1988*
assemblage of photographs, memory map,
story, and driftwood.

This is Stripe Island. This is where the steamer goes along. This is where I used to fish in the summer. And this is where we used to fish after we was married. Tickle in here. This is where we had our traps. And across here, this is the Mark Island. And this is Winsors Harbour over here. And that's the Blind Tickle. And this is what we call the Lighthouse Point. And this is Kanagiktok Bay. Now this is where we used to live, on one of those little islands. It's full of little islands there. Stump Island. And over here Double Island. And this is where the schooners used to fish, some of them. And Coupling Island. And this is Tinker Island. And this is Flagstaff Tickle. And the Railroad Islands, four or five islands all together. And Hopedale of course. It's thirty miles from out here up to the bottom of The Bay, where we used to live. There's another bay comes in between that. Adlatok Bay. And Little Bay. And Ugjoktok Bay. This is the ship's run. This is where we used to live in the summer, to Hare Island. I've been all over the place, see, good many times. There's a lot of islands I haven't got on there. No wood on the islands. Only place you get a bit of wood is where you go ashore and pick it up off the beach. Driftwood. Comes out from the rivers and drives ashore with the wind. All the rind would be gone off of it. When we'd get short of wood, we'd collect it off the shore. Saw them up.

Hilda Dickers, Labrador 1988
assemblage of photographs, memory map,
and story. Collection: Canada Council Art
Bank.

I was born in 1910 in Kanagiktok. It's a very very pretty place. It's a forest of trees. Oh that was beautiful my dear. I love that place. John would come down here to Hopedale to go to the shop in March, by dog team. And leave me alone. Say we was getting short of coal oil, lamp oil. Or we might be getting short of tea or sugar. And there was nothing I enjoyed any better my dear. And I'd go in the woods and all the trees was like arms around me. The trees was like company. I didn't feel alone. That's how I felt. I felt safe. Yes, beautiful, beautiful. This is the place where we lived. When you sees the woods my dear, you'll know you're getting handy to Kanagiktok Bay.

George Flowers, Labrador 1988
assemblage of photographs, memory map,
and story.

That's the kind of place I was reared up. If you heard a noise it would only be your own dogs, or the wind, or birds. And rivers of course. Very very quiet. You could say lonely. No planes, no choppers, no speed boats. This was the only thing growing up, hunting, fishing and trapping. There was no one bothering you. Let me tell you now. You know these Settlers. Let me say this. What they call Settlers, most all of them were reared up in the bays here around the coast of Labrador and now they live in the communities. That's the head of The Bay. Long Point. The Island. Jack's Brook. Little reef of rocks. Fox Cove. The Bar. Stag Island. Tomahawk Island. Scurvy Grass Island and Scurvy Grass Bight. Then it leads on over so far and you turns up to Flowers Bay. Too bad you don't see the hills. I have it all in my experience but I just don't know how to mark it. Nobody would know what that is except for me. Boy if I was a drawer I'd put the hills down too.

Chesley Flowers, Labrador 1988
assemblage of photographs, memory map,
and story.

I went to Hebron once with a map like that. By dog team. He only marked the big islands, and the rattles he marked black. Open water there. Three days going from here by dog team. The land looks different coming back, if you only look straight ahead, if you don't look behind when you're going up.

The Distance Between Two Points is Measured in Memories, Labrador 1988, constitutes a major stage for Marlene Creates in the development of a work which the typology of art history classifies as Land Art (more appropriately described, perhaps, as Art in the Land).

There are eighteen assemblages in this series, each comprising four images: a photograph of an elderly person in a kitchen or living room, a hand-drawn geographical map, a printed text in sans-serif type and, finally, a photograph of a site. The formats are identical (28x36 cm). The two photographic images, the map-drawing and the text create the somewhat abstract effect of two white panels between two black panels. On the floor, in front of each assemblage, with the exception of five, is placed an object of "natural" origin (mineral or vegetable), like a trace of life and/or a quiet clue. Together, the sequences of images on the walls and the compact massing at ground level of the small objects produce a sensation of intimacy that has something slightly austere about it, inviting the spectator to careful observation.

Marlene Creates accurately calls these series "memory maps". The present series concerns memories of recently urbanized inhabitants of communities in Northern Labrador: Inuit, Naskapi Innu, and Settlers of Euro-Canadian descent. They express what has remained engraved in their memories about a place they once lived in, through a map-drawing and a story. These are accompanied by a photograph of the subject in his or her present daily surroundings, while the remembered place is shown as it was when caught by the artist's camera in 1988. The objects placed on the floor (a log, a piece of wood with a bolt in it, a block of pink and black-veined granite, a piece of Labradorite, a square of mossy earth, a round grey stone . . .) are there because they are mentioned in the stories as once having had roles in the remembered places. These objects are not artificial representations created for an art gallery.

Standing in front of these eighteen memory maps, we share eighteen human destinies, as well as the aesthetic and ethical adventure of the artist, who takes her many potential visitors beyond the limits set by ignorance or indifference. The strength of the memories of Clara and Jim Voisey, Joe Ford, Josephine Kalleo, Sam Winters, Hilda and John Dickers, Philip Hunter or Sybilla Nitsman, Rosie and Chesley Webb or again of Chesley and George Flowers, Gilbert Rich, Joachim Nui, Mary Ann Noah, Bert Saunders and Sidney Dicker arises from their experiences of passing from one way of life to another, a process which illuminates the images of the past, rendering them sublime. Through the drawings and stories, the subjects' hunting, fishing and trapping territories, their domestic spaces, and the areas for gathering 'country food' become once again real places of warmth and freedom. Sidney Dicker remembers Nain: "This place here at one time was all green with lots of little flowers. We call them buttercups those little yellow flowers. And all the little brooks were clean. But since they started building it's ruined. When it blows hard we get a lot of sand."

The assembled series are not to be approached simply. Each category of image — room, map, text, site — connects us to a specific domain; at the same time they are indissociable from one another. Our eyes wander back and forth even while we are looking at one image in particular. Marlene Creates succeeds in sharing with us the play of memories of long ago, rooted in pre-urban spaces. These memories are falsely thought to belong to a world other than our own, yet they are so close!

The photographs of domestic spaces show the material furnishings of daily life, both functional and decorative: the cookstove, the refrigerator, the wood stove, the table covered with a cloth, the wall shelves, the spice cupboard, the chest of drawers, the TV, the transistor . . . We see domestic utensils: pots, dishes, plates, glasses, coffee pot . . . Many ornaments are displayed: potted plants, dried flowers, calendars, maps, boxes, figurines . . . Innumerable family photographs, the formats and frames of which might be discussed in terms of their play of visual variations, cover walls and shelves, sometimes on either side of a wall clock or standing clock. The aesthetic status of the clock is ambiguous: it registers time, now imprisoned second by second, while as an object it is loved. The interiors of some of the houses in Nain, Davis Inlet and Hopedale are similar to those of the apartments or residences of working people in urban centres all over the planet.[1] I would like to take longer to identify and situate each object, but for Marlene Creates the images have not been put together for any kind of discourse on the sociology of taste; they are silent witnesses to an overwhelming transformation, the details of which we discover as we go through the series. These arrangements for sedentary comfort do not conceal some upsetting ambiguities in the situation. Gilbert Rich, for example, an inhabitant of Innu origin in new Davis Inlet, has chosen to be shown standing beside his stove, a kettle probably full of water in his hand. He is smiling, a forced or mocking smile? To get water, he has to go out of doors . . .[2]

The hand-drawn maps come after the photographs of the people in their interiors. These maps have the power to fascinate and touch us beyond their status as intense personal testimonies. They probably owe their power to the aesthetic and emotive qualities peculiar to cartography. These qualities can be appreciated throughout the history of cartography, even when the illustrative elements on maps (landscapes, human figures, objects . . .) have been gradually abandoned. It seems these qualities arise out of an ancient will to retrace the exact course of an itinerary, inventing conventional and abstract signs in the process. The oscillation between pictorial representation and abstraction still continues. These map-drawings are both memoirs and imaginary creations.

The eighteen memory maps drawn by the elderly people with whom the artist had conversations resemble (for this writer) fragile linear constructions on white spaces that connote the infinite.[3] But in this case, the background formed by a white rectangle of paper holds a very specific local space. What we take to be the infinite is only the surroundings of a place whose dimensions are both increased and made more precise by the operation of memory. The infinite has become a place travelled through. It is the ocean and the fishing territory. It is the hunting grounds for caribou, fox, and mink. The wood-cutting areas as well. The indented shoreline and the little islands all known by name (mostly Inuktitut). Then at the centre are the houses of family and neighbours. Hills, woods, and rocks are absorbed by lines that describe the relation between the land and the water. As in a group exhibition of abstract expressionist paintings, the map-drawings, at first, seem similar. As soon as we look at them closely, though, we see their differences. Some are complex and seem to bring to life the experiences of a lost geography; others are mere traces, slender unbroken threads indicating small-scale scattered places. Some are more illustrative, characterized by the illusions of pictorial representation. Sometimes writing is added as an aid to memory.

The practice of cartography is part of the graphic tradition of the Inuit. Leaving aside traditional topographic representations from the pre-historic period and considering only the geographic drawings which have been conserved, published or exhibited since the end of the last century, the skill of the inhabitants of the Arctic in situating themselves in relation to the four points of the compass is generally acknowledged. In this regard, Robin McGrath is quite right to remind us of the experiences of Franz Boas and Robert Flaherty.[4] In particular, he associates the current renaissance of Inuit cartography with the negotiations for their territorial rights, which "have required the knowledge and expertise of Inuit elders in documenting land use and occupancy by producing maps to show traditional hunting areas, animal migration routes, sea-ice trails and seasonal habitations."[5] Study projects on land use and occupancy have been underway since 1973, not only with the Inuit, but also, among others, the Naskapi-Montagnais and the Settlers of Labrador.[6]

The danger would be to ethnologize these spatial representations. What struck Marlene Creates was that it is not possible, *for the time being*, to associate certain types of drawing with Inuit authors, others with the Innu, and still others with the Settlers. Expression of contours, isolation of small masses, effects of continuity, simplification or concern for detail, all seem, with one exception, to have more to do with gender specificity than they do with ethnic background. For these people, now removed from the places of their childhood (and often of their adult life as well), the things which retain substance in their memories have to do with geography and work patterns. The differences seem to coincide with practices common either to men or to women. The men (with the exception of Bert Saunders, who gives a detailed description of Old Davis Inlet, the former Hudson's Bay Company post managed by his father and grandfather) describe their hunting and fishing grounds. They draw long stretches of land and water. The women describe a territory defined by activities centred around the house and within a more limited geographic area.

Each map illustrates and enlarges on the text that follows it. It is a visualization of the narrative as the lines trace the life story. Each text replaces a voice. The cold type of the text is fascinating in its contradictions. We hear the echo of a living voice while we feel the weight of dead letters! But the over-all effect of the four images is to make us feel the presence of the narrator. The places brought into existence in the maps live in the stories, but the two are really parallel, so the text could just as well have preceded the map. Jim Voisey is talking and we read, "Now this will be The Bay . . . Nineteen miles of it . . . Island here . . . Island there. Tabor Island where they gets the Labradorite from . . . You'll see what they call Brown's River. But it's only a little brook . . . This would be Garland Bight . . . This is a hill . . . Now off of the Harbour there's islands. One, two, three . . ."

Rosie Webb for her part narrows down her space: "Old man's house here. Path up to our house. And Jim's house up here. Our house. And Ronald's. And Henry's little old house there . . ."

The last images of the series are those of the remembered places. Marlene Creates took these photographs during the second stage of her work: journeys beyond the three communities to the places evoked by memory. Her idea was to follow the itineraries drawn on the maps and to find the significant, remembered points indicated on the maps. There can be no doubt that her experience in doing this lies at the very heart of her piece. The maps and narrative texts come to life at the sites she visited but now it is the memory of a concerned and understanding visitor that takes the place of the memories of the former inhabitants.

The spectator looking at these images in a gallery — the stretches of water, the indented contours of land, the configurations of rock, the masses of forest, the hills, the sky, the horizon lines, the tiny islands and the abandoned houses — cannot help but compare them to the rooms and their furnishings in Nain, Davis Inlet and Hopedale. The piece of Labradorite placed on the floor in front of Jim Voisey's series, or the frame of dried buttercups in Sidney Dicker's series, or again the square of mossy earth placed at ground level in Rosie Webb's series, all seem to be detached parts of the texts and memory-photographs.

The eighteen memory maps of Labrador dating from 1988 are not the first that Marlene Creates has exhibited. In 1987 at Sault Ste. Marie she presented four installations under the same title based on the experiences of elders (men and women) from that region, some of whom are of Ojibwa origin.[7] This was an outdoor exhibit, with the memory maps engraved on pieces of slate according to the original drawings. Another version of this same series was later shown in Ottawa.[8] Then in 1989 the eighteen Labrador assemblages were exhibited in St. John's.[9]

If these works based on memory maps are a turning point in the work of Marlene Creates as a Land Art artist, it is important to understand what this turning point consists of and to ask ourselves if it can be thought of in terms of a more general development in this art form, one which perhaps reveals present-day issues and options.

Marlene Creates' Labrador projects are a consolidation of the Sault Ste. Marie work. Together they could be said to mark a new development in her naturalist expeditions where discreet landscape interventions were characteristic in her way of working between 1979 and 1987.[10] She would go on solitary explorations of geographies and geologies, leaving faint aesthetic traces of her presence which were caught photographically. Her projects were organized visually in a way which respected the memories attached to the places she visited and with an anxious attention to the ambiguities involved in any reference to memory. These projects included the ephemeral application of rice paper, the carrying of rocks and stones, the flattening of wild grasses by her sleeping body, the nocturnal throwing of a stone into the water . . . "The land is important to me, but even more important is the idea that it becomes a 'place' because someone has been there," she was saying as early as 1985, in connection with her project, *Traverser deux rivières: des lieux, des sentiers, des souvenirs.* (Crossing Two Rivers: Places, Paths, Memories).[11] In this quote she suggests that her personal relationship to the environment (seen as the universe or the cosmos) is being replaced by the experience of *particular people* linked to particular places (seen as the spaces occupied by others' lives).

This is not the place to enter into the ideological complexity of the various categories of Land Art,[12] but the work of Marlene Creates could be said to belong to a type that includes, among others, the works of Richard Long and Hamish Fulton, classified respectively by Mark Rosenthal as "Modest Gestures in the Landscape" and "Idealized Landscape".[13] In these works, "Nature" is scarcely or not at all touched and it is the long, slow movement of the body on the earth that creates a sort of communion (or the restoration of a lost relationship!) between the site and the loving and thoughtful walker.

It seems to this writer that the current solitary journeys of Marlene Creates point to a change in these ways of thinking. Generally speaking, many Land Art activities over the past twenty years have been chiefly concerned with basing their visual expressions on cultural attitudes towards nature, seen as landscape. Human beings appeared only in the traces they left behind: either ancient traces (monuments) or traces fabricated by the artists themselves. Marlene Creates has ceased to be this kind of privileged witness because she has sought more relevant witnesses, ones seldom consulted. She has decided to listen to the elderly people of Labrador because their experience — the transition from a way of life inscribed in the landscape to what has become an obligatory participation in urban society — gives life and meaning to those "lost relationships" with time and space which certain land artists have been trying to track down.

At the beginning of the 1990s, at a time when the crisis created by ecological change and attempts to meet it are part of our daily lives, and when, too, the bastions of Western culture seem to be under siege, not so much from other dominant ideologies as from groups of people seeking equal status within revised political structures, it would be interesting to see whether new directions are discernible in the work of certain land artists of the '60s and '70s. It is not impossible for certain practices to be continued, almost

unaltered, because their quality and relevance have not been affected by time.[14]
Furthermore, some of the works produced in the early years of land art could perfectly well
have been created today, under the pressure of contemporary events. A good example, in
my opinion, would be *Time Landscape* by Alan Sonfist, begun in 1965.[15]

In her current work, Marlene Creates has adopted an aesthetic practice which valorizes
the inhabitants of a chosen place and it is their memory that she places at the centre of an
experience of the environment.

But this is not all that she does. Marlene Creates helps us discover places which bear
witness to the scandal created by the colonial system and by post-industrial marketing of
the earth's resources. Are there not among the Innu of the Quebec-Labrador peninsula,
hunters who have carried on a traditional nomad life, their legal rights unrecognized by a
government which in 1970 — without any prior discussion or any subsequent real
compensation — constructed a dam, flooding land on which they depended for survival?
Are we not near or even within the boundaries of *Nitassinan* (Our Land), the territory
subjected to low-altitude supersonic training flights by military jets from the NATO base at
Goose Bay?

Looking at the places of memory and once again travelling the distance separating them
from the kitchens and dining rooms of today, the spectator cannot escape the urgent
reflections that Marlene Creates wants to bring about by means of a visual ordering which
shows the clarity and restraint characteristic of her art. These images have the value of
things shared.

Jacqueline Fry

Translated from the French by Elizabeth Ritchie.

NOTES

1. I cannot help thinking of the narrator of a novel by Dominique Fernandez who remembers the day when a school friend took him home " . . . un trois pièces propre et soigné du côté de Javel. La famille se tenait dans la cuisine-salle à manger, autour d'une table ronde couverte d'une toile cireé à fleurs . . . Moi qui avait grandi au milieu des livres je n'aperçus au mur que des cartes postales, un coucou suisse, le calendrier des postes . . ." (. . . a neat and clean three-room apartment in the direction of Javel. The family was gathered in the kitchen-dining room, at a round table covered with a flowered oilcloth. . . who had grown up surrounded by books saw on the wall only post cards, a Swiss cuckoo clock, the Post Office calendar. . .) (l'*Etoile Rose*, Grasset, 1978, p. 41).

2. In another photograph, Joachim Nui has put up his tent near the front of his house. There, he says, he can find the fresh air he misses and the smell of spruce boughs lining the floor of the tent. In this case the present place and the place of memory are joined together in an attempt to correct the new order.

3. I have written "had conversations" and not "interviewed" because we are not dealing with a sociological investigation in any sense of the term. We are probably closer here to an anthropological experience. It would be necessary to make learned and possibly useful distinctions between ethnologist, anthropologist, artist-anthropologist, and just artist!

4. Robin McGrath, "Maps as Metaphor: One hundred years of Inuit cartography", *Inuit Art Quarterly*, Spring 1988, Vol. 3, No. 1, p. 6.

5. Ibid., p. 6.

6. Hugh Brody, *Maps and Dreams: A Journey into the Lives and Lands of the Beaver Indians of North West Canada*, Chapter 10, "The Indians' Maps".

7. *The Distance Between Two Points is Measured in Memories, Sault Ste. Marie 1987,* "Sans Démarcation", Ontario-Quebec exchange, Sault Ste. Marie, Ontario (through the Art Gallery of Algoma and Visual Arts Ontario), 1987.

8. Gallery 101, October 1987.

9. *Maskunow: A Trail A Path*, Art Gallery of Memorial University of Newfoundland, February 24-April 9, 1989, a group exhibition curated by Joan Borsa, (including six memory map assemblages of Labrador, three by women and three by men); *The Distance Between Two Points is Measured in Memories, Labrador 1988*, Eastern Edge Gallery, April 9-May 25, 1989 (twelve works from the series).

10. In *Overlay: Contemporary Art and the Art of Prehistory*, Pantheon Books, New York, 1983, when discussing modifications of megaliths, Lucy R. Lippard quotes and illustrates *Paper Over the Turlough Hill Cairn, Ireland 1981* by Marlene Creates. Lucy R. Lippard puts emphasis in her note on the local myth that gives the place its ancient specificity but the concerns of the artist were elsewhere.

11. Axe Néo-7, Hull, Quebec.

12. See on this subject Alan Sonfist, ed. *Art in the Land: A Critical Anthology of Environmental Art*, E.P. Dutton Inc., New York, 1983, 274 p.

13. Ibid., pp. 66 and 68.

14. Heidi Geraets, who is preparing an M.A. thesis, *Back to Nature? Land Reclamation and/or Nature Valorization*, is confronted with these questions, particularly in dealing with the more recent productions of Nancy Holt, Robert Morris and Michael Singer. She draws our attention to a series of works on paper by Richard Long, *Untitled* (1987). "His *Untitled* works show a series of footsteps spiralling inward from the edge of the paper until they reach the centre, from where they have nowhere to go." (John Grande, "Art in the Environment", *Discussion*, Spring 1989, Vol. 8, No. 1, p. 8, Montreal). It is important to know that these prints are made by his feet wearing boots that have been dipped in the polluted mud of a river!

15. Alan Sonfist has recreated a fragment of forest belonging to a type dating from pre-Colonial times, i.e. from before the colonization of North America, by planting a large rectangle with indigenous species of trees in La Guardia Place, Manhattan, New York.

ACKNOWLEDGEMENTS

Most of all I would like to thank the friends I made in northern Labrador whose memories form the heart of the work in this exhibition. The Inuit, the Innu, and the Settlers I met generously shared their history and knowledge with me and made my field work a fascinating and moving experience. My greatest debt is to them.

For their considerable assistance in the production and exhibition of the work, I extend my thanks to:
Karen Love, Presentation House Gallery
Patricia Grattan, Art Gallery of Memorial University of Newfoundland
Jacqueline Fry, Ottawa
Justin Wonnacott, Ottawa
Patrick Ryan, Air Canada Cargo Manager for Newfoundland and Labrador
The Canada Council
The Newfoundland and Labrador Arts Council
Multiculturalism Canada

Marlene Creates